The Art of Customer Service

PALMETTO
PUBLISHING
Charleston, SC
www.PalmettoPublishing.com

Copyright © 2024 by Patrick Sanchez

All rights reserved

No portion of this book may be reproduced, stored in a retrieval system, or transmitted in any form by any means-electronic, mechanical, photocopy, recording, or other-except for brief quotations in printed reviews, without prior permission of the author.

Paperback ISBN: 979-8-8229-5075-7

The Art of Customer Service

Understanding the best techniques for customer service

Patrick Sanchez

For Sebastian & Sofia

TABLE OF CONTENTS

Introduction		1
Chapter 1	It All Begins at the Top	3
Chapter 2	Connecting	5
Chapter 3	Customer Expectations	7
Chapter 4	The Closing Always Show Gratitude	9
Chapter 5	The Customer Isn't Always Right	11
Chapter 6	Reward Your Loyal Customers	13
Chapter 7	Nourish Your Employees	15
Chapter 8	Marketability	17
Chapter 9	Safety and Security	19
Chapter 10	The Wrap Up	21
Author Bio		22

INTRODUCTION

The art of customer service. Customer service, serving people, talking to people—for it to be a pleasant experience, or comfortably unpleasant, it's like a white canvas; when using the right brushes and colors, it can create beautiful art.

Feeling good and making people feel good generate good energy. Good energy comes back to you.

There shouldn't be a place of business where the customer doesn't come out feeling good.

After all, life is about feeling good.

The customer isn't always right. However, you should always be righteous to the customer. Treat others like you would like to be treated, or better.

Art begins inside and is expressed outwardly. Treating or serving people begins inside and manifests outside.

Hopefully this book serves as a guide or a reminder of positive humanism and embracing the fellow man.

CHAPTER 1
It All Begins at the Top

If a home is dysfunctional, look at the parents. If the parents are not in unison or in a positive state of mind, organized or happy, those feelings will filter down to the rest of the household.

You can't expect your employees to conduct themselves in a happy, friendly, courteous, and organized way if the leaders on top don't reflect that.

Training and educating are fundamental. Energy is contagious and it travels. Keep it positive; keep it healthy.

Don't always blame the waiter; it might be the manager.

To lead people, walk behind them.

—Lau Tzu

CHAPTER 2

Connecting

Smiling and greeting generally soften people. Every person you approach is a new beginning. Move on from the previous experience. A new opportunity can create a better experience, satisfaction or both. Empathize where necessary. Tone of voice is very important.

You are always networking. Every new person you meet could be the bridge you need to get to the other side. So always leave a good impression.

Remember, it's not their job to remember you. It's your job to be remembered in a good way.

Your energy introduces you before you can speak.

CHAPTER 3

Customer Expectations

When assisting a customer with a request, always listen carefully. Ask questions if necessary. Suggest alternatives and follow through. If a request is not available, offer an option and show samples.

Organization and cleanliness are important to any business establishment.

First impressions, last.

CHAPTER 4

The Closing— Always Show Gratitude

Upon completion of your customer's request, always be thankful to them for choosing your establishment.

Ask them to visit again, but more importantly, give them something back.

If you're a restaurant owner, a small dessert, a snack, or even a free drink would do the job. If you are at an office place, consider a T-shirt, a souvenir, or even a gift card.

No matter how bad or good the experience was, it's 90 percent guaranteed this will cause a boost of warmth and gratitude.

They will come back or refer someone to you. Closing is not just about *Here's the bill* or *Here's how much you owe*. It's about *Thank you for choosing us…please come back!*

Wear gratitude like a cloak and it will feed every corner of your life.

—Rumi

CHAPTER 5

The Customer Isn't Always Right

How do you deal with a difficult or irate customer?

You've done everything possible to please them and to make them happy, but nothing works?

First, apologize, and (if possible) provide some sort of credit.

Have the manager come to your aid to provide apologies and explanations also.

If the customer becomes totally belligerent, have the manager come to your aid.

If needed, possibly ban the customer from the establishment and give a full credit back or offer something next time they visit.

There are people that can never be fully satisfied or happy. Sometimes it's best to let them go.

Remember, never take it personally. Stay professional, stay polite. *They go low, you go high.*

*In a world of chaos,
staying calm is a superpower.*

CHAPTER 6

Reward Your Loyal Customers

A reward is a *Thank you for continuously using my business.* Every manager or owner should recognize this and give back to their customers.

A reward is also somewhat a recognition, and people love recognition and being gifted. No matter how small the reward is, it would make them feel good.

Here are some ideas—depending on your business—to reward with:

Hotel or banking business: Credit the customer with a dollar amount if they achieved a certain balance or if they've been with a company for a number of years.

Restaurant: One free meal a year or limited free drinks (for one day).

My favorite: the owner or the manager gathers ten of their loyal customers (once a year) and has a dinner party for them.

Here, the manager has a conversation with his loyal customers on how they can improve as a business. As a manager or owner, you should take suggestions from those loyal customers and analyze those ideas.

It's not happiness that brings us gratitude. It's gratitude that brings us happiness.

CHAPTER 7

Nourish Your Employees

A stable employee will stay with you for at least one year, and a loyal employee will stay for several years.

However, an employee, like anyone else, needs human nourishment and motivation to stay. Establish good benefits and decent salaries, and have out-of-the-box benefits for employees that have been with you for over one year.

Get involved with your employees. Know about their lives and aspirations, and have a relationship with them.

Remind your employees to use their benefits appropriately.

Have sit-downs and meetings once a month. Remember to take suggestions from your employees.

A healthy employee equals a healthy company.

"When given enough nourishment and care, anything can grow."

CHAPTER 8

Marketability

Having a successful business requires promotion and good marketability.

Use social media. It's free and reaches thousands of people. Take pictures of your products, your place, and your staff.

Make sure your place is always kept up clean; it makes an impression.

Always check your bathrooms. Make sure your staff looks good and presentable. Remember light attracts light.

A brand is no longer what we tell the customer it is. It is what customers tell each other.

—Scott Cook

CHAPTER 9

Safety and Security

Unfortunately, given the world we live in, we always have to be aware of our surroundings. People from all walks of life may carry negative experiences or traumas. If these individuals are "triggered" in some way, they may want to "act it out" in your place of business.

Make an effort to have video cameras in your establishment. Train your staff in CPR techniques and, if possible, self-defense.

> *Knowing is not enough,*
> *we MUST apply.*
> *Willing is not enough,*
> *we must DO.*
>
> —Bruce Lee

CHAPTER 10

The Wrap Up

Customer service is about establishing and maintaining positive relationships with our customers.

It's impossible to manage a business if you can't develop good working relationships with staff. That relationship transfers over to the customer. Avoid focusing on micromanaging and neglecting the macrocosmic goal. Your business depends on the people under you, the ones that face the customers and deliver their requests.

Customer service should be a business of making people feel good.

A well-executed customer encourages customers for life.

—Shep Hyken

AUTHOR BIO

Patrick Sanchez, a native New Yorker with roots in Florida and the Dominican Republic, brings a wealth of knowledge from his diverse professional background spanning over 35 years. His experience in the financial, legal, and call center industries has honed his customer service skills, emphasizing the importance of serving others for business success. His understanding of customer service, drawn from these varied sectors, forms the foundation of his book, 'The Art of Customer Service.' Patrick's expertise offers valuable insights to those seeking to enhance their customer service skills, making his book a must-read for professionals in this field.

www.ingramcontent.com/pod-product-compliance
Lightning Source LLC
LaVergne TN
LVHW051926060526
838201LV00062B/4715